THE MISUNDERSTOOD JOURNEY

A Memoir

THE MISUNDERSTOOD JOURNEY

A Memoir

Darren W. Phelps

Copyright © 2020 Darren W. Phelps
All rights reserved. No part of this book may be reproduced or transmitted in any form or by any means, electronic or mechanical, including photocopy, recording, or by any information storage and retrieval system with the exception of a reviewer who may quote brief passages in a review to be printed in a blog, newspaper or magazine without written permission from the author. Address inquiries to: www.DrDarrenPhelps.com

Scriptures references are NIV translation unless otherwise noted.
Published with assistance from Expected End Entertainment
ISBN: 978-1-7344101-2-9

Printed in the United States of America

CONTENTS

	INTRODUCTION	1
CHAPTER 1	LIFE CAN BE HELL	7
CHAPTER 2	I'M PREACHING MY WAY OUT	23
CHAPTER 3	LORD, YOU SAID WHAT?	39
CHAPTER 4	AFTER	55
CHAPTER 5	I SEE SOMETHING	63
CHAPTER 6	LOOKING IN THE MIRROR	77
CHAPTER 7	GIVING UP IS NOT AN OPTION	85
	ABOUT THE AUTHOR	95

DEDICATION

William Henderson, my cherished friend – more like a brother for many years. My deepest regret is that you transitioned before seeing this book. May your soul rest in peace and strength!

Direck Lee Phelps, my only brother... the oldest, lover of animals, sports, and laughter. I hope you are looking down at me and proud of your brother! I love and miss you deeply! Ma sends her love.

ACKNOWLEDGMENTS

There's an endless list of people that I'll love to thank for the successful completion of this book. On top of this endless list is Augustine O. Ojeh for his editorial support and for keeping close track, ensuring that I met every deadline. Tarvoris Adams Carnell Creative, LLC www.carnellcreative.com for his creative book cover illustration and website design, C. Nathaniel Brown, Expected End Entertainment www.ex3ent.com for their professional publishing services.

I'll like to thank my Mother for her unselfish love, strength, and for not giving up! You have always been my biggest cheerleader! To my daughters Joscellyn and Whitney. I am extremely proud of your gifts and achievements. Our love and bond are one of my greatest gifts. To Rev James Ross and Rev. Steven Tate your unwavering friendship, prayers and encouragement provided me with unmeasurable courage! To Peggy Shorey, your listening ear, experiencing our "rough" seasons together with truth and justice provided me with renewed hope! To Rev. Allen Harris, your pastoral care was critical to me not giving up! To my Christian Church (Disciples of Christ) family, the place where God blessed me to grow, explore, and to allow God to use many of my untapped gifts. I love my church! Also, my acknowledgment goes to every clergy person that is going through tough challenges in their personal life that is often unspoken. To the readers of this book, also, I'm most *honored and I hope that I've impacted your life positively through my experience.*

Thank you and keep pressing!
—Darren W. Phelps

INTRODUCTION

Looks may be deceptive because the strongest people barely look half as strong as they actually are. Many times, I've shared my life's stories to certain audiences. Those who heard me talk resolved that I'm resilient. Although I may not describe myself that way, I believe that we become myopic when we try to stare through ourselves.

I know that everybody fights their own demons. My story is not special or exceptional. However, I believe people who read this book will find the strength that they've yearned for. If you think the world is closing in on you, this book will show you there are no boundaries in our world. Our potential is limitless, but we can only reach the greatest heights if we keep striving.

Are you erratic or do people think you're irrational? Do you find it hard to fit into the world around you? Are you standing at the fence seeing others become who you desire to be? Whatever the case, you're not alone.

As I share my experiences in this book, I'm confident you will find yourself somewhere in my journey. It will trigger some of your own journey experiences and you will find reasons not to give up on yourself. You exist with a God-given purpose and have an identity for which you must stand firmly. It is okay to not have your life figured out. It is perfectly okay to be on a rough edge. It's okay to be on a journey, even if others don't understand it.

A fellow preacher once said to me, "Darren, you always act as though God will always bring you through all your difficulties." In public, I always appear to be winning the fight. I never get discouraged, openly. The truth is when you are living life as a misunderstood journey, not all the information about you will be out for the world to know. You must deal with some inner fears behind closed doors, on your knees, and with God.

Most of us believe that showing our vulnerabilities as humans make us appear weak. I was once scared of showing my weaknesses in public while soaking my pillows when alone. But giving up is the last thing that should come to mind in this adventurous life. With breath in you, there's no way giving up is justifiable. More often than we want, life reveals our faces to experiences that we never knew existed.

Your story is unique and may have taken a different road from mine. You may have experienced more tough moments in life than I ever did. Perhaps you are experiencing one as you read this book. Regardless of the intensity and type of challenge, there's an 'after', a joyous stage of life that comes after the long-endured rainfall.

As you live, you give energy to the people around you. You love people in the best way you can, although you may not know how to show it. Often, you don't receive the same energy that you give. Still, you wear a cheerful smile, believing that everything will be fine. I am imploring you to hold on to that belief because everything will be fine.

Why is it so difficult to see through the smiles and

energy that people carry? Why don't we see the burdens that are weighing on their minds and sending undue wrinkles to their faces? Perhaps, that is why we are human. We're perfectly created beings filled with our own imperfections.

As you move through life, remember that our journeys are often misunderstood. Don't expect people to understand your challenges the way you do. But hold on to the people you love and build a good relationship with your family.

My story as young boy in Queens exposed the lapses in my relationship with my siblings. It shines light on the deep feelings that young children carry when the family bond they crave is missing.

Our life's callings are brought upon us in the most unexpected places. As David was called upon by Samuel from the bushes, you might also be called upon from your deepest troubles. I'm going to share the story of how I met Mary, the woman who was called to usher me into several life-changing encounters.

Life changes can also make us think that we have been with the wrong people for a long time. This may not be true. Meeting Carol, whom I would go on to marry, was the best part of my life. Although things didn't completely work out with us, she made great impacts in my life, for which I'm grateful.

THE MISUNDERSTOOD JOURNEY

The story of the man at the Pool of Bethesda is one that resonates with me closely. Many times, I wonder how the man got to the pool. He must have left his house believing, just like everyone else, that one day, he will reach his destination and he will find the help he needs. Indeed, he made it to the pool and found the healing he never knew existed. It was exactly what he needed.

From a relatively young age, about 16, I've moved relentlessly to find my own "Pool of Bethesda", in spite of the challenges. In this book, you will look at life's deepest lows through my lenses, including the loss of a family member through a divorce, ministerial hostilities, a troubling self-discovery journey, and life-threatening health challenges. Amid the low moments, there have been high moments that are worth cherishing with those I love most, my kids and their kids. They kept me going, allowing me to be here to share my story and to pursue the calling of God on my life to serve people and advocate, educate and be a liaison for people have been overlooked, marginalized, and have lost their voices along their journey.

As you read this book, I pray that you get that same resolve to never give up on yourself, on life, and on your vision, even though there might be things that you can't explain to those around you.

Follow me through my misunderstood journey, and with God by your side, I believe you will come to peace with yourself and your misunderstood journey. Just as Paul stated, we must press towards the mark of the high calling of God.

CHAPTER ONE

LIFE CAN BE HELL

> *"Being unwanted, unloved, uncared for by everybody, I think that is a much greater hunger, a much greater poverty than the person who has nothing to eat."*
>
> — **Mother Teresa**

Most of my childhood experiences can be explained in one phrase: "Life can be Hell".

I grew up in Queens, New York, with tons of emotional baggage coupled with environmental distortion. From the grotesque streets of Queens, I developed a mindset that I still carry with me. Those experiences convinced me that the influence of our upbringing have a lasting impression on us.

For a young boy of color in the heart of New York, challenges within my family, my environment, and my schools, made life almost unbearable. Some of those challenges are beyond describable; they are better felt than said.

Hell is defined as a place of destruction, torture, and isolation. It comes with a feeling of constant pain and unresolved conflict, within and without; a place that fertilizes our tears and pain.

Growing up, I did not have the verbiage to express

these constant feelings of pain and fear. It was beyond my understanding. Many kids in the neighborhood were in the same situation. However, none of us could predict the intensity of one another's struggles.

My mother, a strong woman, was one of my greatest blessings. Young and single with little support, she raised my brother Direck, my sister Gwen, and me fervently. She had several difficulties settling down and finding a man to love. Marital challenges were on the rise in the late '60s and '70s, years after Nancy Reagan pushed an unfair divorce in 1948, and her husband, President Ronald Reagan, signed the "no-fault divorce bill" in California in 1969. Most people, uncertain about the future, were skeptical about getting into marital entanglement.

Regardless of obvious difficulties, my mother's efforts were rewarded by short term relationships with overmatured boys, i.e. boys with men's physique and age. From those years, I learned that age didn't qualify a boy to become a man. I saw full-grown men act incredibly childish and abusive. My young life was affected by my exposure to these people and more.

Drifting between men, my mother's life was volatile. My siblings and I were not left out as we traveled through the same unending emotional rollercoasters. "Men" with different principles and varying levels of immaturity made it hard to find a male mentor to look up to, or at least, a young man with the vibrance to stand upon his shoulder. Who am I to complain about men not being stable with Mom? What about my birth father?

My birth father has always been (and may remain) an area of my life that I don't discuss, for personal reasons. However, my love remains with him. His absence from my life – our lives — exposed us to several episodes of domestic violence. On the sideline with my siblings, we witnessed Mom suffer bouts of physical and mental abuse from the various men that entered and exited her life.

One incident that stuck to my memory happened on a cold New York night. Just before dinner time, Mom and Charles, my sister's father, were having a misunderstanding. Gwen watched her father transform into a monster that she couldn't help but loathe. He tried to set us ablaze. Who knows why a misunderstanding would stir such aggression?

I saw the terror in Mom's eyes and the fear in my sister's. I felt horrified, furious, and broken. Gwen and I hid Mom in the closet in my room as Direck watched in awe as Charles gathered toilet tissues and a gas can to burn us in the house. Charles shuttled across the house at a pace we had never seen. Motionless and dumbfounded, I watched the episode unfold, resolving not to let Mom get into another violent attack.

Charles unrolled and spattered the tissue papers around the apartment, intending to light them up once he was done. We were all in there – three kids and a woman. It was terrifying and paralyzing.

Once he stepped outside, perhaps in search of something, we ran out the house and made it to a neighbor's house. We hid in the neighbor's house, terror-struck and wordless. We never ate that evening's dinner. The stains from that night never left me. At such tender ages, we witnessed it, felt it, and carried it all our lives in abject silence.
Mom immediately transitioned into a more confusing phase of her life.

"Try to make the marriage work," many women advised her, including my grandmother, who I watched apply ice to my mother's face. Many people thought we were too young to know what was going on. We were young but not too young to know that we were unhappy and unsafe. We lived in a terror synonymous with hell-like teeth-gnashing.

Mom was determined to make her marriage work. She was willing to put up with the endless mess from a frequently drunk and abusive man. The 'make it work' mentality of most women became Mom's biggest adversary. Sadly, my grandmother and other women in the neighborhood believed that having a home was far more important than her sanity and that of her three kids. "You have a home," I heard them say to Mom. I wondered how having a home was worth perennial suffering. Indeed, life can be hell!

Some of the most challenging parts of my personal life had interpersonal relationships at its core. Relationship challenges with my two siblings built a gap between us. We fought every time we had differences. Dialogue was not a recognized option. Being the middle of three children with extreme personalities, kind of made it challenging for me to sort our differences. No matter how hard I tried, building a rapport and bonding with Direck and Gwen were often met with severe roadblocks.

I craved strong family bonds. I still do. Meeting friends that shared a strong bond with their siblings stings me every time. I wished I could relate with Gwen and Direck at least half as much as my friends did with their siblings. Well, wishes are not horses; they never were and never will be.

Queens, in the 1970s, had a population of around 2 million people. Attending a public school as a black kid was a daunting task, especially when most of the teachers and other students were white. During integration, there were just a few black kids in these white schools. It was almost impossible to socialize. With every conversation, the stigmatization and segregation screamed louder. We had a rough time blending into the educational system. Mom, on the other hand, was determined to give us the very best education possible, irrespective of the underlying challenges. Skin color and the worst financial crisis wouldn't shift her commitment to giving us the best.

PS176 Queens, now recognized as The Ovington School, wasn't the best of schools at the time but I am grateful to have attended. My siblings and I would travel to school and back home together. As quiet as the journeys to school were, they were memorable. There were times I spent with people that really cared about me regardless of the frequent frictions between us. This apparent togetherness continued through intermediate school (Mid-School, as it's known). We spent the years at Springfield Gardens (I.S.059) together until high school.

Direck and Gwen found Andrew Jackson High School more appealing. I still don't know why. However, spending my early adolescent years in Benjamin Cardozo High School seemed like a good fit for me. The school boasted of their diversity practices, especially those years when inclusion and diversity were a fresh craze. Also, Bayside wasn't such too far, and walking down for classes alone was no challenge.

Because the diversity craze was beginning and most families of color were unsure of how things would play out, I was often the only black boy in my class and one of the few in the entire school. The teachers and other students were wary of us. They didn't know what to do with us.

They called us "Negro", "Colored", and "Black," instead of acknowledging our given names. They were words made from letters of the Greek alphabet. So were our names. As a kid, it was hard to understand why they didn't address us by our names. Darren wasn't so tough to pronounce, was it?

The experiences were awful. Today, I realize that kids are mentally magnetic with those early-age metallic experiences sticking and shaping their lives. My exposure to those conversations influenced my thinking, esteem, and consequently, how I relate with my immediate environment.

Of all high school experiences, my third-grade memories were carved in stone. Mrs. Bowdine, third grade teacher at P.S. 176 asked us to stand outside with our backs against the wall. Black boys only.

"I have enough of *these*," the teacher said to another teacher. The teacher's tone was disdainful and soul-piercing.

Was she referring to all the boys in his class? Has she had enough of boys? Why were the Black boys standing with their backs against the wall?

"These!" She referred to a group of colored third graders as "these". I listened in silence and confusion.

Mom was angry when I told her about the incident at the end of that day. For years, I didn't know what the teacher meant and why Mom was angry. However, those experiences, unknowing to me, were shaping how I viewed myself in the eyes of others. Self-esteem, they'd call it but who knew?

As the realization of her loathe for Blacks came upon me even as a young boy, I found her repulsive. I acted up in her classes. They weren't interesting to me anymore and her questions directed towards me and other black kids in the class screamed, "Negro!"

Naïve, I found it rewarding to act disrespectful towards her whenever the opportunity presented itself. Although quiet with my siblings and fighting with them, memories of that experience weigh on my self-esteem. Like it is in the core of boundless infernos of brimstones and sulfur, I screamed inside my soul for help, a sting of life's hell.

Third grade went through regardless of the challenges with the white teachers. Then, came fourth grade. Mrs. Catherine Obarski is a notable Fourth Grade teacher that never left my head. She's a force to be reckoned with.

My first week in fourth grade started a remarkable phase of my life. An afternoon with Mrs. Obarski and Mom turned things around for a while. While she spoke with Mom, I stood close listening to their conversation. Admirably, these two women discussed the interests of a young boy that was just two feet away from them. Knowing of my hellish attitude and the fact that I was listening to adults converse, my new fourth grade teacher pulled me by the collar. Her grip was firm and my resistance wasn't worth calling that at all.

"I'm not having this in my room. Understand?" Her voice was firm and piercing, but somehow appealing. Like a recruit would respond to his first command in the Navy Seal, I locked eyes with my silent mother briefly and returned my stare to this assertive teacher that seemed to have me figured out.

"Yes, Mrs. Obarski." My response was cold and harmless as usual, contradicting the reputation I'd earned from the previous grade.

"You are a good child and you will do well. I expect you to be at the top of my class," she said to me in a tone that brought my guards down.

That was the first time someone believed in me. She acknowledged a part of me that was hiding behind the mask that the environment had forced on me. Indeed, it takes a discerning eye to see the heaven in those dwelling in their self-defined hell.

I experienced a shift in emotions at school, became more respectful to my teachers, and learning was more efficient than it ever was. However, my home life remained complex with the friction between my siblings and me increasing and repeated domestic violence experiences. With Mom and my stepdad being out of resources frequently, we'd go home with worries of living the weekend without gas, electricity, or both.

Con Edison, powering New York for decades at the time, never had it easy at our home. Electricity distribution in the mid-20th century was not as sophisticated as it is now. It really didn't change for several decades.

Thrilling episodes unfolded every time they came around to disconnect our services. One evening, Con Edison came to shut off our power. I was standing beside the power meter, trying to prevent them from shutting it off. These officials, technicians, and engineers seemed helpless against a teenage boy. Meanwhile, Mom would scurry to their office trying to get an extension, which she did most of the time. I don't know how she did it, but it was magical.

Mom was a superwoman, always juggling multiple tasks on any given day. With more endeavors than I can possibly imagine, life's hell and 'mid-century New York' gnawing at her, she ensured we got the parental care that she could afford. With every opportunity presented, she taught us indelible lessons of survival. Her strength and resolve were admirable.

The source of her resilience is not unknown. Mom was raised in Harlem by her grandparents, Rev. William Robinson and Jackie Robinson. They were one of the memorable parts of our lives. Grandpa Bill and Grandma Jackie, as we lovingly called them, were strong, feisty, loving, selfless, and wise. They were our great grandparents, nonetheless. Grandpa Bill managed one of the The People's Community Church, which still exists today. They'd lived at the top floor of the Harlem brownstone and the congregation gathered in the hall on the lower level.

In every believer's heart, regardless of religion, life's hell breaks in the place of worship. Remembering church services in those years come with bliss. Homemade cakes, kisses from members leaving lipstick stains on my cheeks that made me flush crimson, and shuttling to the corner stores with other kids were pleasant memories worth keeping.

In this hell of a life, however, sweet memories are complemented by sad ones. Perhaps that's why they are sweet memories in the first place. Mom and I drove to

Harlem in her orange Vega to visit Grandpa Bill. She had been trying to reach him for days. Cell phones were not a thing at the time. The mailman did most of the reaching out or you just had to go knock the doors of those you want to reach out to. Landlines were available, however. Mom just couldn't reach Grandpa Bill and she's worried.

When we arrived at his apartment in Harlem, we met him lying on the floor, lifeless, and gripping a yellow phone. My throat instantly went dry. Mom pulled away from me, scurrying towards him. I don't remember her shouting or panicking. She seemed to have everything under control as she pulled the phone from his grip, planted a kiss on his cheek, and turned to me as I stood behind her, almost nonexistent.

"Go sit on the couch and watch TV, Darren," she said. Although her voice was calm, it pierced the deepest layer of my heart. From where I was sitting in the living room, I saw a full view of Grandpa Bill's body. My mind raced indistinctly. Boy oh boy, how hard it was to find the words to say!

What's going on? I wondered. Mouth agape. My eyes fixed at Grandpa Bill and Mom, as she expertly put him together. She picked up the yellow phone, dialed numbers, and the news about Grandpa Bill's passing on flew out to everyone she could reach.

A few hours later, the funeral home arrived. She rubbed my shoulder softly and took me to another room where I sat cluelessly. I peeped through to see as they put Grandpa Bill in a body bag. As disheartening as this could be, Mom was focused and resilient. I never saw a tear roll down her face. Indirectly, she taught me to manage my emotions during a crisis regardless of the magnitude. However, there's a difference between dealing with emotions and hiding them. This, I learned after several years and will detail in succeeding chapters.

This misunderstood journey had been from my childhood. At parties, barbecues, and social events, I had smiles on. While playing handball and checkers at Cambria Heights Park, shopping at Corvettes, and getting ice cream at Co-Op City, I looked cheerful. It's hard to tell that those smiles were far from authentic. Who would have guessed that a young innocent boy had his bed and pillow located in the heart of hell?

Underlying the laughter and smiles were severe pain, bitterness, anger, self-loathing, and silent, incessant cursing. My mother's infectious strength was critical for survival at those times. It has always been. She's incredible, never giving up and always staying real. Her strength was inspiring. *You dare not be a weakling when Momma's never backing down!*

Industrious, she'd turn pots of spam and noodles into

meals. Exuding strength above her natural weaknesses, she made sure we never saw her fall prey to her crushing emotions. However, I caught her sob herself to sleep several times. We shared that in common, we always did. I'd sob above the comfort of my pillows, releasing all vulnerability in the absence of everyone. Then, we all breezed through the day relentlessly.

Without denying any of it, she's the reason why I'm this bold and swerve through storms even in the most unexpected times. She's responsible for my stubbornness to circumstances and she's well aware of that. From her, I learned that crying was perfectly okay but never to be engaged in public. Cry in private because the tear glands are there for a reason. Thereafter, like chess pieces on a chessboard, stand tearless, and determined in the world.

Not allowing people to see your vulnerability, however, has its downsides. According to my family belief, crying is for punks and weaklings. In our endless attempt to avoid showing our vulnerability, we were silent about everything that happened in our lives. The tension grew in silence. As we held everything in, our lives were impacted in several ways that we were oblivious of.

Several decades past and I've learned that holding this in for too long negatively impacts your relationships with others. Transparency, although not a default for me, is a proven recipe for metallic relationships.

At every moment in our lives, we are driven by desires. My desire as a child was that all of life's hell came to an abrupt end. I wanted to take a piss. Nobody seemed to be noticing anything as events unfolded. Nobody was saying anything about the events. *Are these things not worth discussing?* I've wondered time and time again. Of course, they are but nobody was saying anything, still.

Life can be hell regardless of your origin, skin color, religion, and gender. The friction between my siblings and me, my extended relatives, friends, and teachers contributed to the sad memories of my childhood. Our struggle with poverty may be responsible for these challenges. Although Mom did her best, it was unbearable. I needed to get away from the grotesqueness of my life, family, education, and everything. I was in my own Angry Red Planet and I wanted to flip the channel.

CHAPTER TWO

I'M PREACHING MY WAY OUT

"When we allow ourselves to be vulnerable, we are not pretending, we are not hiding – we are simply present with whatever is going on inside us. Ironically, it is this very feeling of authenticity that draws people to us, not the brittle effort of perfection."

Maureen Cooper

At an early age, I began to have deep conversations with myself. I tried to figure out where I was and why everything was happening to me. My childhood seemed to have been plagued with one gut-wrenching situation after another. The crisis I experienced pushed me to the brink of giving up. I needed to run away from all these horrible crises. The burden had become too much to carry. My entire body began to snap in response to my internal struggles.

The reality is that all these things were happening at once. At 13, the situations were overwhelming. I was drowning. Discovering my life's purpose wasn't forthcoming. Understanding life was almost impossible for me. Well, it is for virtually everyone because it's a mystery. I had tough questions to ask, but who would answer them? No one was talking.

Gradually, I lost the ability to express my pains. I

needed a positive outlet in which to pour everything. I'd concluded that life had set me up for perennial failure. I resolved that nature loved others more than it did me. Without counsel of any sort, I decided to run away. Of course, bringing my worries didn't make sense. I was hoping I'd find some people to talk to.

One illustration that struck was the man at the Pool of Bethesda. It seemed to me, at the time, that my life was taking the same shape as this man's. Wonders filled my young, naïve mind when I thought about him. What was he doing at the pool? Was he running from something? Did he leave a place of struggle, hoping to find solace at the pool?

That was Young Darren concluding that we need to be at the right place in time to receive our breakthrough. Running away meant that I was going to my Bethesda, hoping to find answers to the deep questions that flooded my mind and to find someone that would listen and talk about life. I mean, real life, the one that evidenced our vulnerabilities. I thought that maybe, only maybe, I'd find hope if I left the tense confines. I believed that things couldn't be worse if I found myself in a new place. I sought newness of surroundings, one I wouldn't have had if I remained fixed in the same position.

Packing and goodbyes are for planned journeys. With only a bag in hand and no goodbyes, I sneaked out of our house on 218th Street to Linden Boulevard. That was it... my long-craved escape to something new and exciting. Frustrated to the bone marrow, I had no clue what I was doing. No plans or whatsoever. To keep moving was the best thing to do. Actually, it was the only option I had offered myself. My first goal as a fugitive was to reach the new McDonalds for a happy meal. That could've been my last happy meal or the first of many more happy meals. There was only one way to find out: KEEP MOVING!

I felt pains that taking long lonely walks only magnified. And there I was magnifying and synchronizing with my pains. Those were the most uncertain moments of my life. It was a hard call, parallel emotions waging wars against themselves on the battlefield of my mind. The growing conflict within me was enough to cripple me on the track. I was hungry, distressed, angry, confused, and lost. I kept moving, nonetheless. I was moving in any direction that would take me farther from home.

Looking back to that day, I'm most grateful to God for giving me the courage to make that decision and the strength to stride those paths regardless of the struggles within me. I'm convinced that He had plans for me because that journey, albeit misunderstood, was the first of my many divine encounters. He set the way for me and met me on the road. Indeed, we must "continue to work out our salvation in trembling and fear". We can neither do this in comfort nor in a familiar place of trouble. We must move to work things out.

As I walked through the streets far from my house, I hadn't resolved my destination. Would I be heading back home? If I would, when would that be? The vacuum in my heart grew more prominent. I needed to speak to someone to feel happy. I needed food. Dogs barked and kids played with skateboards across the street. Their laughter was admirable, but they seemed to be the least of my concern. I needed to come up with a plan. Viable or not, I should have one. Mom always did.

I resigned to the corner of a house fenced with metal. The gate was made of metal bars and kids played harmlessly inside the yard and play area. Their smiles were a reflection of the joy they felt inside. Unlike mine, their grins were full, and they were flexible. I couldn't help but stare at them through the bar gate in admiration. They looked like they never had a second of worry since their birth. Oh, God!

While I interacted with the kids through the gate, a lady came out of the main door of the house and approached me. "Who are you?" she questioned. Several other questions followed as she calmly investigated my identity. I answered all her questions with the fewest words possible. One-word answers were always handy to me, especially when I was absent-minded. When she noticed that my attention was on the kids playing, she opened her gate and asked me to join the kids. Unbelievable!

In New York at that time, no one literally opened their door to a stranger, not to mention a strange black teenager. Her warmth was divine. "Mary," I'd call her for the sake of discretion.

After hours of escape from my worries, playing with the kids, she offered me a chair at her table. She offered me food. She made me a cup of tea. It was hot, and just as Grandma Jackie would make it for us when she was alive. She'd add evaporated milk and take a soft sip before handing the cup of tea to us. Mary refreshed the loving memory of Grandma Jackie with her angelic gesture.

While we sat at her table, we had a long conversation. She told me a few things about herself. She was a teacher and managed a childcare center right in her house. Apparently, I'd been in her childcare class for a couple of hours being cared for. She loved working with children although she had her own much older children. She was happily married and a minister at a local church. Her transparency towards me broke the walls that I'd built up over the years. To every question she asked this time around, I was detailed and vulnerable. However, she ensured that we didn't go into too many details. "You're welcome to my house at any time, Darren," she said in an attempt to close the conversation. Being able to speak freely and express my brokenness to 'Mary' without fear of being seen as weak meant a lot to me. The conversation was therapeutic. Like the man at the Pool of Bethesda, that was my breakthrough.

My walk back home that evening took a 180-degree flip from what it was earlier that day. My thoughts were futuristic and hopeful. My focus shifted from the aimless, undirected teenager to a desire to teach and serve. The thought of serving created a sense of value for me. It kindled something within me that I didn't understand as a kid, but I was excited about something for the first time. That was all that mattered to me. Truly, as Jaggi Vasudev asserts, "excitement is life happening intensely and we must all be excited to feel alive".

I frequented Mary's home. I'd spend most of my free time there, playing with the kids, and having deep conversations with her. She'd ask me real questions, and I felt safe to express everything that was locked up inside. One day, she asked about my life's experiences. She was warm, and I didn't see any reason to hold back the things going on in my life. I was a mess, and someone was willing to listen to me tell it all. Although I was just a high school kid, she understood that I had my ups and downs in life. She believed that experiences had more to do with situations and backgrounds than it did with age and educational levels.

As I poured out my experiences to her, I broke into

tears. For the first time, I was crying in the presence of someone, not with my pillows. It was hard to let the tears roll but much harder to hold them back. So, I let them do their will. They poured and I sobbed with a clotted throat. I had carried the knapsack of burdens for so long that I didn't even know how heavy they were anymore.

"Come to church with us on Sunday," she said to me amid my tears. Her invitation sounded alien to me because no one had ever invited me to a church or anywhere. Even though Grandpa Bill was a pastor at the People's Community Church, my parents didn't make church services a part of their routine. We attended churches only when there were major events like Easter and funerals. We never did the regular Sunday services, nor did we imagine that churches had a reason to meet any other day of the week.

The service at the Cathedral that following Sunday was miraculous. The environment was the warmest place I'd ever been. God was preached with an unparalleled enthusiasm that infected me. I grew curious, wanting to know more of the things I never thought existed. The music was one I cannot forget. The Cathedral was filled with a spirit that welcomed me. Although the spirit was new, it felt familiar, like it had been a part of me long before my birth. I'd tried to explain the feeling, but words didn't come close. Perhaps, I'd find something if I looked outside the Greek alphabets. I didn't know what was happening, and I cried. I was fully clothed yet felt naked and unashamed.

I've heard people talk about God. Grandpa Bill didn't stop talking about Him. However, I've felt that those were nothing beyond fanaticism or some sort of myth that no one would really understand, yet a few followed dumbly. It turned out I knew nothing and couldn't see beyond what my iris permitted. In the church that Sunday, everything changed. Looking back at those days, I wonder how God does His wonders. Thirteen years of grotesqueness began to take shape in just a few days. Snap!

A few years later, the Cathedral hosted a revival with Rev. Browning as the guest speaker. I'd heard of Rev. Browning several times. Sometimes, Grandpa Bill spoke fondly of him. I'd wondered what was so special about him. During the revival, which Mary invited me, I understood why my great-grandfather was proud of him. He was dynamic, and his preaching was piercing. At the time, I heard only his voice speaking to the congregation until his message began to penetrate my soul. His preaching exposed to me the parts of me that I had no idea was existential. As he spoke to the crowd, I broke down. With my hands up and tears pouring down, I felt like a wailing toddler, unable to understand nor explain the reasons behind my tears. Deep down, I could tell that there was nothing hidden in me. Not anymore. I was unwrapped and lay bare yet as confident as I could ever be about my transparency.

As the sermon heated up and my heart poured itself through my tears, I noticed Rev. Browning walking through the crowd. He stopped in the aisle where I was seated. He gestured to the senior pastor and the other ministers to come over.
"This boy has a calling to preach in his life," he said to the ministers and senior pastor. I wondered who he was referring to. I looked around to find the person and he pointed at me. He approached me and the ministers followed. As he drew closer to me, my legs quaked, and my eyes flooded my face. Softly, he touched my shoulder and I lost all hold of myself, falling to the floor.

I struggled to get back to my feet but I was helpless. I could barely feel the floor, and at the same time, I wished it wasn't there. I stole a glance at the people around me. Mary and her family were excited. Everyone seemed to already know about this calling but me. How did they? Not the right time to ask questions. *I must get back on my feet quickly*, I thought.

As I stood, I felt defeated and completely powerless about my situation. I cried. Like a neonate, I wailed and broke further. They returned to me moments later. I'm not certain how long they had let me be. Maybe five minutes. Maybe 20. But there they were again, gathering to pray for me. And with another contact from Rev. Browning, I went out again, this time under the pews. I crashed to the floor and everything seemed to go out. Time lost its essence and I lay there motionless. Tears rolled down the sides of my face. As they trailed the skin on the sides of my face, I felt its warmth washing the specks of dust from my eyes and carrying with them the worries and fears that had overwhelmed me for years.

That was the beginning of my journey through salvation. God began speaking to me and revealing more of Himself to me from that day through dreams and visions. He guided me on how I could live my life in ministry. My whole world changed from that encounter and I faced the reality that I had gone through all those difficult situations in preparation for the responsibilities ahead. What I'd always wondered, however, was if my parents had to be in that situation just to provide the perfect nesting for my transformation.

Perhaps, I won't get an answer to that question because God cares so little about our past. Rather, He is more interested in the things he has designed us to do. We are not in the right position to question the situations that we had gone through. We are, however, obligated to seek clarity of purpose from him every time we have reasons to question our direction, even before a reason for questioning arises.

My first official sermon was an event to remember. It

was the best of sermons. As a matter of fact, it was not an impressive one. I was nervous and unsure if I was sending the right message. I was worried about facing the public and speaking. Little naïve Darren was going to preach to a congregation. He was going to teach them about God.

Prior to the sermon, I took the time to prepare the message and had notes written on the index card in my file. "The Least You Can Do". The topic still resonates with me. At every point in my life, I wonder the least things I can do to enhance the life of others – physically, emotionally, morally, and spiritually.

The delivery that day was an epic failure. The message was unclear to the listeners. And maybe it was boring because my nerves took a stronger hold on me. However, the church and the people around me supported me as a young minister. They gave me a 'pass'. That was my first pass ever. The first time I was given a pat on the shoulder for doing something poorly. The smiles on their faces after the sermon, although certain that I didn't do well enough, expressed their confidence. That meant a lot. With people believing in me, pouring my heart into ministry was easier. I was grateful.

The love that the church showed me gave me a reason to strive to become better. I wondered how I'd combine my scattered past with an organized ministry. I was unsure how I'd get rid of my past struggles and embrace this new calling that God had placed on me. It's one thing to know where to go and it's another to leave where you've always been.

Amid my wonders, God revealed to me in a way so subtle that I found it impossible to misunderstand or question. The closest description I could give to His message at that time was: "I am not asking you to divorce yourself from your pain. I'm not asking you to deny the existence of the events and the tragedies that you've been through. I'm asking you to use them, tap into them, call it into purpose, speak it, and call life into those dead and hard places."

Indeed, I was journeying a misunderstood path, and nothing has been clear without God.

The instructions stuck and it was my responsibility to work it out. I moved with the same charisma that I always had. A smile on my face and a suit on my body made people think I had it all figured out. I attended church services with all diligence. At most events, revivals, and services held at the local church, I arrived earlier and left later than most attendees. I was pouring it all.

The choir made trips to other churches for ministry and I was right with them, learning and serving. I was going all-in, supporting the youth and young adult church I was an active part of. If our pastors had to speak at a different church on any day, I was with them, learning and serving. No part of me was left behind on this journey, albeit misunderstood in every facet.

While I struggled to make peace with myself and find a way to tap into my experiences as instructed, I did my best to serve. I struggled with finding this balance until a minister gave me what I'd refer to as the deepest piece of advice then.

"You've got to preach to yourself. If you don't preach to yourself, you can't get free from the pains. You can't get past whatever you've been going through. And then surely, your preaching will never be authentic," the minister said to me with construable precision. From that day, I made sure that I spoke to myself. I preached to myself more than I did to others. I taught myself, calling life into the hard places within me. As I preached to myself, I shared those personal sermons that God instructed me to share with the public.

This brought a clearer sense of purpose to me than what I had initially. Instead of preaching my way out of my troubles, I came to peace with myself, tapped into my experiences, and the misunderstandings in my life, then poured myself totally into every sermon that I took. That was authentic. It is great to live what you preach. So, being able to tell it how it really was brought me closer to identifying my purpose as a young preacher. Preaching doesn't only expose the things we have hidden within us, it also brings peace to the mind of everyone involved. Being unauthentic has always reflected in the lives of the listeners because your message doesn't connect with your spirit. You're called to build a connection with them and until you are totally connected to the message you preach, the bond may not fully form.

The opportunities the church presented to me are among the many things I am grateful for. One Sunday at the church, after I had begun my journey as a teacher and servant of the Word, I met the lady named Carol. Still a teenager, she lived a few blocks away from mine on 227th Street. Her mother had brought her in to register for our Youth Retreat that year.
She was familiar and we had connected before. We'd met in fourth grade when I was playing on her father's baseball team. However, there was something about her that Sunday that took over me. From the table where I was seated, I saw her smile light the room. While her mom completed the registration, I couldn't help but stare at her in admiration. She was simply beautiful.

Carol was a strong person, spiritual and gentle. As I investigated her briefly, I discovered that she attended August Martin High School and was a member of the track team. She was filled with an understanding of the ministry that exceeded mine. I was relatively new to the whole church role.

From those early years in ministry, Carol was helpful as we both served in the young adult ministry. Our story is better told in later chapters of this book. However, it is noting now that her wisdom and strength complimented me as I continued seeking God and His instructions.

CHAPTER THREE

LORD, YOU SAID WHAT?

"Love does not begin and end the way we seem to think it does. Love is a battle, love is a war; love is a growing up."

James A. Baldwin

High school was filled with exciting activities. It's ironic that amid those exciting extra-curricular engagements in school, I didn't get excited before my decision to leave the house. The adventures were almost endless. I was a leader in the Key Club, a volunteer at the local YMCA Children's Program, and worked at Mary's Love Childcare Center after school hours. The hilarious part of high school was the network of friends that I kept. Most of my friends were from wealthy backgrounds. While I rode two NYC buses to make it to school every day, my friends were driven to school by their parents and sometimes, they were allowed to drive themselves. It was exciting to have friends with taste. I admired them and wanted their life. However, I wasn't ready to take any big leap out of my jurisdiction. I had resolved to follow God's lead and wait for his appointed time.

While I balanced schooling, work and ministry effortlessly, Carol and I were getting along. We started dating my junior year. With her charming smile, she had seized my attention. Beyond describable beauty, Carol was tall with long legs and unusual laughter. Enchanted by her personality, I found myself staring at her as she navigated unfamiliar spaces. As we bonded, we did almost everything together. We prayed and shared ideas. I was in love with her and everyone in the church knew it. It was too difficult to hide and they loved us. Our connection was eminent, and everyone expected us to get married.

For several years that we dated, Carol and were celibate, showing each other an unparalleled level of respect. On a New Year's Eve, I went on my knees and proposed to her. It was nothing fancy, just the usual young adult boy asking a young adult girl to spend the rest of her life with him. The New Year's Eve service was full in the youth church and everyone was present when I proposed. My heart raced for a moment hoping that she wanted me as much as I wanted her. It didn't take a minute, however, and her response came out as a buoyant, "Yes!". Amazing! Carol was willing to be my wife and I could go head over heels to make it come through.

The following year, with Carol still in high school as a senior, I moved to Petersburg, Va., to attend the Virginia State University. Like most other relationships of the type, challenges came with the transition. Blame it on distance or maybe on the fact that we were so fond of ourselves, but we had one challenge after another. We argued and saw several differences between us while we spoke over the phone. Notwithstanding the challenges, we never cut communication. We utilized every means possible to keep touch and connect with each other.

Resolving endless conflicts was demoralizing to me but what wouldn't you do for the person you love. Carol had made me feel truly valued by fellow humans. I believed that she was God's gift to me and a guide to propel me into a promising future. With this belief undeterred, I sought God for my next move. I prayed intensively and took counseling sessions with our youth pastor. After that, I decided to walk down the aisle with Carol in hand.

While we planned our marriage, Carol's mom sent me a letter, expressing, with great candor, her disapproval of our marriage. Although I would have loved to have kept this piece of opinion to myself, keeping vital information from Carol a few weeks from our wedding day was not a good promise of respect and happy marriage. Carol had several heated arguments with her mom about her disapproval. Believing that everything would fall into place and she'd come along soon enough, I didn't take their heat to heart. Needless to say, their differences stood firm longer than I anticipated.

July 11, 1987, Carol and I got married at the Cathedral despite of the storm hovering over our heads. It was a day to remember for so many reasons. The extremely warm weather was one irking reason to keep that day in mind. It was so hot that the church service was filled with hand fans flipping faces and positions. My white tuxedo made room for some air to touch my body and reduce the sweat pouring out of my skin. Nobody wants to be sweating so heavily on such an important day of his life. My best man, Glen, stood beside me with confidence. His confidence in me warmed my feet more than the weather did. It didn't take long before I was staring at Carol as her father walked her down the aisle towards the altar.

The reception was held at Mary's. We could not be more grateful to her for her support. She'd been more than a friend to me; she's been a coach and a cheerleader. She complimented my mother in ways that weren't her strongest. By the time we got to the reception venue, some of the food was spoiled, thanks to the extreme weather. Nevertheless, it was a memorable day for both Carol and me.

Our honeymoon was in Canajoharie, NY. It wasn't anywhere like the usual honeymoon we read about. We had neither a dream wedding nor a dream honeymoon. In Canajoharie, I worked as a camp counselor to raise money to take care of some of the bills which weren't extravagant since we spent the two weeks in a small cabin outdoors.

After our honeymoon, we moved to Petersburg, Va., where I continued my university education. Carol decided to attend Hampton University, which wasn't a very far trip from where we lived. While we tried to fit in new waters, I continued to explore what I believed God had called me to do in ministry. I was struggling to let myself loose of the past experiences and struggling to accept being a part of ministry. Although things were coming together slowly, there was a battle within me that I had to settle. So, I preached to myself every day. The learning curve was steep and long. Carol and I had to adjust to marriage, relocating, and trying to make sense of ministry, while dealing with the challenges of building a new home, schooling, and working to pay the bills. Still young, we were forced into maturity. Homesickness was one of the things we needed to deal with quickly. Managing finances wasn't a joke by the slightest thought of it.

While we dated, we had an endless flow of love and joy, even with the challenges. After we got married, things shifted, rocking our relationship to its core. Everything changed and we struggled to restore what we had before that hot July afternoon. Perhaps, marriage was a serious step that we were underprepared for. Quite unfortunately, the counseling that we received from senior pastors and others didn't do much. They didn't offer solid guidance on becoming one in marriage. Carol and I lived as two distinct people. We were more friends than a couple. We lacked the understanding required to consolidate the friendship, partnership, and all there is to marriage outside the fun. It created a vacuum between us. We craved for true love. I wanted a sound and whole marriage with a titanium bond because I believed that marriage was a lifetime commitment.

During most of our heated arguments, Carol expressed her desire for intimacy. It wasn't very familiar to me at the time. Looking back to our numerous arguments as I write this book, I understand better what she desired. No excuses for depriving her of all she longed for. Her honest requests to have more of me sounded alien to me at the time. I didn't grow with a family that showed intimacy. We were robot-built and we didn't see a need to connect with ourselves. Unlike me, Carol was a part of a family that openly expressed their love for each other. She had a strong connection with her siblings and parents. She must have seen her parents be intimate and admired that. I understand now that even if she didn't get the best of marriages, she wanted one in which she would connect with her husband far better than she ever did with her siblings.

We didn't know how to fight safely. Growing up, I left the dangerous fights with my siblings. I didn't imagine myself getting physical with my wife. However, the arguments we had were intense. They left deep emotional wounds that never healed. We never discussed any of the wounds or tried remedying them. We left them untended and more wounds were created with each new argument. Our expectations were unrealistic. Better said, they were misconstrued. We couldn't seek counseling and mentorship. We wandered ignorantly through marriage, expressing our frustrations, and disappointments in the ways we knew. More times than I'd counted, I wondered what caused the great divide between us.

These challenges, however, were not getting in the way of ministry. I loved ministry more than I did my wife. She knew that and I still don't know how she accepted that. Being from a God-fearing home, she probably understood what it meant to us to follow our calling in ministry. While we struggled to fit into our marriage life and manage our young home, God was faithful, opening doors to help me further my ministry. One day, in Petersburg, Carol and I met a military couple and began worshiping with them in a local church. One Sunday, we attended the large Baptist Church in the Petersburg, Va. There, the pastor was a singing preacher and the service was captivating. Has there been one that wasn't?

We decided to settle, join, and connect with the large Baptist Church in Petersburg. We attended services and took part in church activities. In no time, I was asked to read scriptures and pray at the pulpit. It was a great honor to be given a responsibility that significant in a large church. Sooner than I thought, I was asked to preach at youth worship services in the area. Because the church was one of the biggest in the area, they announced the service and preacher in the Progress-Index newspaper back then. Every time I saw my name featured in the newspaper, I was excited.

The church loved my "puppet ministry" and they made me realize how much my preaching had improved from the first time I gave a sermon at the Cathedral back in New York. Eventually but unexpectedly, they asked me to serve as their part-time youth pastor. It was an exciting moment in my journey as a young minister. I coordinated children's church, summer camps, and other ministry functions that were within my responsibility. As a part-time pastor, I received a stipend which meant a lot to me and my young family. I got a significant level of excitement that complimented the frustration that I faced from being a young married pastor building a family with a laughable level of experience. All through these times, I still hadn't figured myself out. At every moment along the way, I kept asking, "God, you said what?" I was unsure of what step to take next. I didn't know where to go and what to do next. God has always guided my path and I'm clueless without His direction.

As I served this church, I received invitations to preach in different places. I was honored to have been considered worthy of preaching in most of these churches and gatherings. My schedule was always full since I was working as a part-time youth pastor and revivalist, evangelizing at every opportunity that came my way. I believed that God brought those opportunities my way to give me direction and for me to pursue my ultimate purpose. Every month, I'd serve at the home church in Petersburg for two Sundays. The other days, I was out evangelizing on revivals and honoring invitations at other churches.

Called by the age of 14 and licensed to preach at 16, I knew almost nothing about life outside ministry. I've struggled to make sense of ministry, itself, but God has never given me a reason to think of anything else. Serving and teaching at various locations as God made it possible, I was often drawn aback by my insecurities and the burdens that I carried regarding my marriage, among other things. My inability to create a ministry-life balance was a sore spot in the marriage. My life started in a grotesque environment and it seemed like I was facing yet another grotesque future for myself and my first child who was due the next year.

In the middle of the whirlwind, God revealed to me a vacant church in Dinwiddie, Va. It was the most unexpected revelation that I received as a young pastor. Well, that's why it's a revelation in the first place, isn't it? Visiting the church, they wanted me to serve as their permanent pastor. It's exciting to move from a youth pastor to become the pastor of a two-Sunday-a-month church in Dinwiddie. The congregation was a decent size with an older congregation. The appointment humbled me and most of all, made me nervous.

There were members about my mom's and Grandpa Bill's ages. At 24, I was leading sermons at the church. It was unbelievable and until this moment, I'm not sure how I was able to accomplish it. It was God that got me there and He got me through and through. He never stops getting us through.

With my ordination and consecration in view at 24, I accepted my first church pastorate. The letter I received included an offer for $90 per Sunday, a beeper, AAA card, three-week's vacation, and a hotel room if I needed one. The additional funds and increased ministry responsibilities were instrumental to the growth of my young household.

Prior to my ordination, I realized that the outgoing pastor at the church was in the position for a few years, which offered me a limited time to get in shape. I had to assume the position prematurely. I was the first minister my pastor ordained and to make sure that I was prepared for the ordination before I assumed my new role, he consulted area pastors to get me in line. All the area pastors consulted were men, including Rev. J. Jones, who served as the moderator, and Rev. J. Dugger my mentor.

Rev. Dugger was my 'Drill Sergeant' and he was a tough. We met a few times each week in his den that smelled like a heap of stale cigars. While we were fully engaged in the training process, his wife would serve him dinner. He ensured that I went through all available resources that recorded the doctrines. He'd correct me time and time again. "Boy, you must learn all these to be an effective pastor," he'd say with a stern voice. All his teaching and mentoring played significant roles in preparing me for ordination. However, knowing the doctrines had little to nothing to do with improving my capabilities as an effective pastor.

Because I was bi-vocational during my first call, it was challenging to manage all my commitments. I taught at an elementary school before moving into nonprofit. Thereafter, I dabbled into managing a childcare center as I once resolved after my first visit to Mary's, not because I wanted to pursue the goal of caring for kids. It was mainly because I wanted to have my children close to me. I was so inclined to give them the love that they would need, the one that I never had when I was growing up. I wanted to have that connection with them and make sure they weren't going through the same things I went through. I wanted us to discuss everything. I wanted to know their challenges and how I could help at every moment.

I gave up all that on a Sunday evening in Dinwiddie. There were almost 200 people gathered to witness me walk into the next level of ministry. I had completed the drills from Rev. Dugger and followed instructions as they were revealed to me.

As the ordination went on, I grew nervous, mentally magnifying my deficiencies and shortcomings. Inasmuch as

I don't compare myself with others, I was scared. The responsibilities that come with being an ordained pastor was getting a strong hold on me. Although I felt a need to, I couldn't doubt that God had revealed this to me. They had come upon me stronger than I could resist. I had dreams and visions that were clearer every time. Those times, they were as vivid as vivid can be.

The calling grew stronger and my resistance grew weaker. I knew deep within me that God was calling for something unusual. However, I felt I needed more time to prepare. It was a lot of responsibility to live up to. I wasn't even getting my household in order and was tasked with guiding a congregation. It was nerve-wracking for me as the ordination went on.

"Yes, Lord. Help me, Lord," I prayed silently as the event went on. The flood of emotions splashing against the walls of my mind were unsettling. Even though I wanted to be an evangelist and win souls, I didn't feel equipped to lead and serve the souls that were being assigned to me on that Sunday evening. However, as Rev. Reeves preached, my spirit became peaceful. From his sermon, I was convinced that indeed, God said it and I must fully believe it and accept the responsibility that He's placed upon me regardless of whatever is going on.

As the moment approached, they put a stole on me and the ordaining pastor said, "You carry the burdens of the people, and you pray for them."

I wasn't sure what that meant, but with my hands on the Bible, I simply responded, "Yes." That wasn't the time to ask questions and it was evident that every pastor had given the same answer in their time.

I remember kissing Carol, who was equally saying a big "Yes" to my service. We knew very little of how our 'Yeses' would affect our lives and our matrimony. I didn't know, at the time, that along with the 'Yes' would come sacrifices, pains, rejections, lies, hurts, confusions, internal wars, and church dysfunctions.

My ordination exposed many truths of ministry as well as my theological precepts. My ordination invalidated all the goals, visions, and desires that I had within me. With my ordination, God planted new seeds of hope and purpose in my soul. He re-engineered me to pursue the calling that he had placed upon me.

Still clueless and unknowing of what the future had in store for me, God comforted me saying, "If you go, I will meet you there. If you trust me, I will open up the windows of Heaven. I have anointed you for such a time as this. I'm calling you out, calling you up and calling you to this new work."

The Lord's words are still sealed in my heart and have

guided me throughout this journey.

DARREN PHELPS

CHAPTER FOUR

AFTER

> *"Without a fresh perspective about pain, a compelling vision, a clear plan, every heartache has the potential to stop you in your tracks."*
>
> **Sam Chand**

"After you've suffered a while, I will restore you and make you strong, firm and steadfast." 1 Peter 5:10.

I have preached from and taught from this scripture on many occasions. It was a continuous encouragement and support. It provided hope and comfort to me. Oftentimes, it kept me from going astray and being offended during life's challenges.

Many times during our storms, we forget that "after" will come. While we experience the heat of our battles and try to make sense of it all, we should know that God is preparing for the after.

It suggests an end. It reminds us that all suffering has a date in which we will find rest and peace. Needless to say, my "after" felt delayed and far from reach. My "suffering for a while" seems like years and decades. A new morning should bring new joy. In my experience, the sufferings became common, deep, personal and even expected.

One of my most painful experiences happened to me on Sunday, July 31, 1996. My brother was murdered. I remember that day like it was yesterday. Around 3:00 a.m., my mother called me and screamed, "They got my boy! They got my boy!" Her sobbing, weeping, and screaming startled me. I jumped up trying to get my bearings, thinking it was a nightmare… and it was.

I kept saying, "What?", "No!", and "Not Direck." She was waiting for confirmation from family in New York. Direck was murdered in the Bronx. Two young boys tried to fight him and at some point, one of them got a gun and shot my brother. I can still remember the sound of my mother crying. It was as though from inside, she was screaming for release. My life changed. My soul wept.

I began to doubt that I was experiencing what the scripture shared about "after". My life was flooded with death and challenging experiences. When Direck was murdered, I was a pastor, Carol and I were separated, and we had two young daughters. I was alone when my mother called that early morning. There was no way to process it. I called my pastor and informed him. Since it was Sunday and we had an early service at 8:00 a.m., I went heavy, confused, and alone. The pastor sang Douglass Miller's "My Soul Has Been Anchored". As I write, I am listening to the words of that song:

"Though the storms keep on raging in my life
And sometimes it's hard to tell the night from day
Still that hope that lies within is reassured
As I keep my eyes upon the distant shore
I know He'll lead me safely to

That blessed place He has prepared
But if the storms don't cease
And if the winds keep on blowing in my life
My soul has been anchored in the Lord
Ooh, ooh
I realize that sometimes in this life
We're gonna be tossed by the waves
And the currents that seem so fierce
One thing I like
But in the word of God I've got an anchor, hallelujah
And it keeps me steadfast and unmovable
Despite the tide
But if, if the storms just don't cease
And just in case the wind keeps on blowing
Blowing in my life
My soul
My soul's been anchored
In the Lord"

After the pastor sang, he told the congregation what happened to Direck, and I wept like a little child. My entire body grieved! It was a weight in my chest that I still carry to this day. I didn't even know if the "after" would come.

My mom, sister (Gwen), and I traveled to NYC to identify the body and make final arrangements for Direck. As we arrived to see him prior to any embalming, I tried to convince my mom not to come in; I would go. She insisted. We walked in and the staff greeted us, tried to console us and prepared us for Direck's condition.

No words could ever prepare a mother to see her son dead on a stretcher. We took her hand and walked into the room. My heart was pounding. I had seen my share of dead relatives and friends but not my only brother. We stood as they pulled the curtain back. My nightmare became real. My mom screamed and fell to the floor. Before I could get her up, my sister stormed in the room and followed my mother's emotions. I cried, looking at my brother, and trying to get my mom and sister off the floor. "This is not real. God, where is my 'after'?" I cried bitterly.

Days later, we held the funeral. Rev. Dr. Hazel preached. I was able to meet many of Direck's friends and several of our family were in attendance. I recall having to say something. Surprisingly, Carol was there and sat next to me. It was awkward because we were separated, and our marriage was almost becoming history. She was not really the nurturing type, but she did her best, given the circumstances. That was the first time people asked how I was, and I replied, "Numb!" Truth be told, it was best that way. My many moments of anger and rage were not healthy. I was in a crowded room and felt alone. Repeatedly but silently, I cried again, "God, where is my 'after'?"

I miss my brother deeply, although we did not have a strong connection. At his funeral, many of his friends would tell me how he was talking about me and they shared details of my life. It created a new level of regret. I do not live a life with regrets. Yet, I remained upset that the last time our family saw Direck was at my Aunt Kim's wedding. My absence was due to a lack of funds and trying to hold down a job, church, and spending time with my daughters. I did get to speak to my aunt that day.

Direck was around so I heard his voice. Today, in my home office, I have a picture of him and one of my aunts. It reminds me of that day that I missed the wedding and missed seeing Direck for what would have been the last time. His voice was all that was left. Although our conversations were brief and generic, I always cherished them. How I wish I could go back to that day and have a do-over. Each tragedy taught me that life is not just short, but it's also fast-moving. I miss my brother. When we buried him, he took a part of me with him. "Direck Lee Phelps," I called his name. I kept asking, "Lord, where is my 'after'?"

My experience with death was normal. While in 6th or 7th grade at I.S.059 in Queens, NY, the school office staff called over the sound system and told me to bring my things because my mother was coming to get me. That puzzled me. That never happened. We were latchkey kids so I either walked or rode the city's bus home. I went to the office and sat on a bench behind the long and high counter. No one saw me there. I overheard the staff speaking… "Is Darren on the way? Sad about them finding his father dead." Wait. What? I jumped up on the bench and scared the staff. They called my name and I took off running, busting out the door of the school and running home like a wild child. I was overwhelmed!

Amidst all of that, I felt like I lost everything, including my mind and the struggle to keep my peace. I spent more time trying to figure out what's happening internally with me than really seeking help because I was busy trying to process the fact that all these things were going on and I was required to be strong.

After is defined as a time that is later than some other time. An example of that is when something happens subsequent to something else. This certainly applied to my life's experiences. My question is when is the 'after'? I assumed what is to come would be better than what was, perhaps, just different and less painful to the soul. My waiting and anticipation of my 'after' has created a calm and a stirring in my soul. I longed, sought, and hungered for the 'after'.

It is that pushing and reaching for my 'after' that keeps me waking up with joy and moving through the day. Actually, my firm belief that my after will be better has established a level of defiance towards everything that has been assigned to block my goal, crush my soul, or darken my vision. It's because I know my 'after' is waiting on my arrival. My faith lifts me and carries me from pain to purpose… After! Just after!

DARREN PHELPS

CHAPTER FIVE

I SEE SOMETHING

> *"You are the sum total of everything you've seen, heard, eaten, smelled, been told, forgot – it's all there. Everything influences each of us, and because of that I try to make sure my experiences are positive."*
>
> *Maya Angelou*

In the movie, "The Wiz", the wicked witch asked her servants not to bring her any more bad news. At a point in my misunderstood journey, I could relate to this part of the blockbuster movie. The countless episodes of my sad life and challenging journey were magnified by yet another heartbreaking reality when I was diagnosed with multiple sclerosis.

Juggling divorce and the crises that I was facing in the church was one I was capable of handling but standing up against a disease that was beyond my control can only be God putting His supportive hands upon me. Many things had gone sour at the time. Carol was pushing a divorce vehemently and I was terrified about losing my kids and being locked out. Truth be told, I never lost my faith amid those threats.

While I chased ministry and my spirituality, I was on my way to discovering myself and accepting who I had always been. It was a tough time, I'd say time and time again. The church's revolt, my wife, my kids, my family, my mom, and me. Most importantly, God. Everything was happening too fast and I was overwhelmed, still with no one to speak to about my challenges. Like the dark old days, I was locked up in myself, being weighed down by the worries I carried within me.

In 1998, my vision was affected. I had to visit the clinic for eye examinations. I wondered if I needed new glasses and the ophthalmologist was the only person to determine that. I didn't want my challenges to get in the way of my care for my health, so I visited my regular clinic for a check-up. While I prepared the day of the visit, I felt sluggish. I wondered what was wrong. Unsure, I resolved that it could be the stress of everything.

During my examination at the clinic, the doctor said, "I noticed something in your eyes." That piece of information was scary to me. I wondered what it could be that was in my eyes. I thought it was stress or anxiety. A doctor was seeing something else and it made me panic. I began praying because I was worried about getting sick in a time like that. If anything, I needed my health to carry me through the challenges before me.

The doctor made me go through another series of tests. The results were withheld from me and I was asked to return to the hospital in a couple of weeks. As I made my way home, I pondered about the doctor's statement. What would he have seen in my eyes? It's hard to tell because doctors will not provide any concrete information to patients until they are certain of the diagnosis and that meant a series of tests and weeks of kept appointments.

A couple of weeks passed, and the long-awaited day came. I went back to see the doctor and instead of telling me what he saw in my eyes, he referred me to an optical neurologist at the Medical College of Virginia. It was unbelievable to realize that a routine eye check-up was escalating into an appointment with a neurologist. However, my doctor recommended that I start wearing glasses until I completed my sessions with the neurologist.

For the next few weeks, I struggled to find an open slot in the neurologist's appointment schedule. Eventually, I got a reservation in the last quarter of 1998. Our first meeting was conversational although he asked some unsettling questions about my past. He wanted to know how my parents lived their lives and if they had any medical challenges that had gotten my attention. I was transparent with him about the fact that I didn't really know much about my dad. Nevertheless, I gave him every detail about my mother to the best of my knowledge. The questions he asked included certain symptoms that anyone around the house could have observed but maybe not me.

He confirmed that my doctor saw something during our last examination, but he needed to confirm what it was. To do this, he had to recommend a series of tests for me again. "We will hope for the best," he said to me as he scheduled me for various tests. From that day, I underwent one test after the other. By the time I was done, I had only a pint of energy left in my cardiac reserve.

One of the tests required the extraction of my cerebrospinal fluid (CSF). The collection process was a delicate one and required precision. It's done using a large syringe with a large, scary needle. They inserted the needle through my backbone to draw the fluid that lubricates the spinal cord. The technician collecting the specimen warned me that shaking any of my limbs during the collection process may result in complete paralysis of that area of the body. Since he was trying to steal fluid from an area of the body that had a complex network of nerves, he had to ensure that the needle comes out the same way it went in. That way, it wouldn't distort the normal physiological process. It's a difficult task to stay still and relaxed while experiencing such a painful procedure.

While all this was happening, I never told anyone. My kids wondered what was wrong with me several times, but I stood firm, telling them everything was all right. One time, I blacked out and tripped when I was walking around the house. My kids were concerned and asked what was wrong. To make sure that they didn't know or suspect that anything was wrong, I told them that my dog tripped me while running past. It was an excuse that I felt guilty about, but it was the best I could do to keep the girls from worrying about me.

After the doctor examined the collected sample, he asked me if I had any injuries growing up. Frankly, my youth was turbulent. With Gwen, Direck, and I always fighting and leaving bruises on each other, there were countless records of my childhood injuries.

However, one that I considered detrimental was a big fall that happened while I was much younger. I fell on my head as a kid. I had also consumed a full bottle of aspirin. I can't tell if it was accidental or intentional. I doubt if it's the later because as a conscious child, I had never considered suicide and overdosing could be considered suicidal. I've had several other head traumas during my childhood. I even experienced convulsions. I communicated all these to the doctor without neglecting the symptoms, rashes, and weird stuff that I experienced as a kid.

Traumas and multiple sclerosis were not left out from the pathological experiences that I had as a child. Regardless of the lethargy of these ailments, most of the people around me never knew that Young Darren wasn't all the way healthy. I learned very early how to hide my pain and weakness!

After the doctor shared that he was unable (at that time) to provide a diagnoses, he said I might have multiple sclerosis in my 30s. I lost my inner joy, and the first time, I wondered if my health crisis would cause me to give up on all my dreams. I was clueless. Ignoring my resilience for a moment, I felt like the doctor gave me a death sentence.

Of course, I'd get enough time to spend with my kids and I still had the strength to cater to their needs and fend for myself over a long period. I'm still doing that as I write although these words are being crafted from pains and fatigue. I was worried about so many things including my mobility, the challenge with the church, my speech and my memories. Oh, yes! I worried about having partial or chronic amnesia. Maybe I was overreacting to the diagnosis. I was hit hard by that piece of information.

The doctor talked about several symptoms that I may be experiencing. Because I paid very little attention to my body, I didn't know if I was experiencing them. I had been too focused on the challenges I was facing to pay attention to the things happening in my own body. It's not a reality that I'd wish for anyone but there I was trying to understand my three-decade-old self. I had dismissed several other symptoms that I considered insignificant in the past, however. When you juggle life, sanity, and ministry it can be easy to dismiss minor symptoms, believing that things will get back to normal.

Our bodies are designed to work in a pattern. When things change, the patterns change. Although those changes may be slight and negligible, ignoring them gives them the chance to build up within us to attain a level of malignancy.

Before I left the Medical Center of Virginia that day, the neurologist gave me an instruction. He demanded that I keep account of my body's behavior on a notepad over four to six weeks. This was to ensure that I acquaint myself with the patterns of symptoms in my body. I went home and bought myself a notepad that was always with me. I built a habit of always writing my observations down as I swerved through my day.

After doing my due diligence on the doctor's instruction, I got an appointment slot with him weeks later in the first quarter of 1999. Right in his office, I explained my observations to him. The changes were far more than I had imagined, and it appeared that my body was completely different from what I used to think it was. I underwent another series of tests including a CAT scan, which was painless. "We need another extraction of cerebrospinal fluid, Darren," the neurologist said to me in a calm voice. *That scary procedure again!* I cried silently.

The pain was unbearable as they collected the fluid from my spine. A friend that followed me to the appointment assisted in holding my legs in place to ensure that I didn't shake while the fluid was collected. However, it wasn't an easy fit and I was curious. I cried as the needle drove through my flesh and between my vertebrae. I wondered what could really be wrong. Tears flowed down my face in sadness, and I feared the potential loss of my limbs.

I was almost immobile after the procedure. My friend helped me get dressed and drove me home, leaving the doctor to test the collected samples. He set another appointment with me a couple of weeks out. The nurses in the medical center were warm and cheerful. Indeed, if there's a place to get better in health, it is a hospital where the people treating you are cheerful.

When I returned for my appointment a few weeks later, I met one of the neurologist's nurses in the foyer. She and I had grown familiar with each other throughout the period that I was visiting the medical center. She hugged me as soon as she saw me. That was unusual and made me think that my test results were back, and they weren't good. I shrugged reassuringly, knowing that I was prepared to receive the worst news.

As we entered the doctor's office, he was seated, and we stared at each other brusquely. "Sit down, Darren. Sit right here," he said as he pointed at the seat in front of him. It was unusual because whenever I entered his office before, he asked me to undress.

"Well, we have the results from your tests," he said with a straight face. I gave him a slight smile in return for his professionalism and concern. "I know," I responded. "I have multiple sclerosis."

The nurse looked at me in shock and the doctor nodded his head slowly. Perhaps, he imagined that slow nods would make the reality less piercing. Well, it was glaring enough that I'd be living on medicines for a very long time. Although no one knew what was going on at that moment, I thought it was time to speak to a few people, including my mother, about what was going on.

But while I thought about who else I should break the news to, I wondered what the church would think about me when they found out that I was sick.

How are people going to treat me? I do not want to be pitied but when they know that I'm sick with multiple sclerosis, they may do that.

Will they consider me a weak person? I didn't want that. My thoughts were crippling. I was suddenly drained while I was in the doctor's office. It was such an unhealthy state of mind that I couldn't get rid of as quickly as I'd have loved to.

I called my mother to inform her about my illness. My whole body was in pain. I felt turmoil in my system and there was nothing I could do. The doctor had placed me on some medications that were sickening and drained me. I was losing my mind and often consciousness.

One evening, my mother made her way to Virginia to spend the time with me. I recall her sitting on the couch with my dog. She wept and prayed at the same time as she stared at me across the living space.

For weeks, the medicines kept messing with me and sent me back into that cataclysmic experience, separating me from my surroundings. After every shot of the medication, it took me a long time to regain my composure and react to my environment the traditional way. Eventually, the doctor took me off the medication and offered one that didn't make me sick.

With most of preaching engagements canceled and my post-divorce experience weighing on me, times were tough. My condition didn't allow me to work and get things together. My kids were worried, and I felt bad to have them worry about me. The church had exiled me and there was literally no one to turn to at that time except the people around me, the same people that had always been there... family.

I learned to appreciate life from that moment. My perception of existence changed. I worried less about what people thought of me. I became less concerned about the fact that no one knew or cared about my survival. I picked myself up and headed straight back into the world. Back into ministry, fighting, leading, and serving just as God had instructed me to.

As I navigated yet another blow, I began to believe that multiple sclerosis was the thorn in my flesh. Paul speaks of this in the bible, asking God to remove his thorn 3 times. However, God offers grace that was MORE than sufficient. Truth is, I did not want to hear that my body pains are constant and often intense. I feel it when I move, sleep, eat, sit, or do anything. I feel it when I preach, and I feel it as I write this book. It's so much for me but I won't stop fighting, for I am of few days and full of troubles, but never will I let those troubles define me.

Life went on and the fights became tougher.

Sometimes, I thought I saw something, but nothing was never really there. With my body numb on the left side, it was hard to go on at full pace. The experiences were unbearable. I would feel pricks from my fingers to my toes as I stood or sat. My eyes got blurry and I often lost my vision. With all these, ministry was at the peak of priorities. No one knew what I went through. No one ever felt or saw my pains. They saw me slow down and look tired, but they assumed it was how I was designed, perhaps.

Inasmuch as the doctor saw something in my eyes that day, he had no idea how much of that 'something' I see every day... the pain, anguish and unpredictable symptoms that keep me numb. Indeed, a thorn inhabited my skin.

I have marched, sang, and talked to people about this. I've exposed myself to hundreds or thousands of people, who now have an idea of what it feels like to be in my shoes. Regardless of my exposure, there's a part of me that shakes and gets overwhelmed by nerves when I think of how people would treat me. The times when the people around me felt concerned the most were those days that I was in a fetal position with spasms that made me cry out loud. What is the need to hold back the tears when life smacks you on the butt?

After being diagnosed with multiple sclerosis and living with the pain. I have embraced this situation. Accepting to be new, I'm learning endlessly and equipping myself for the sensitive exposures that are influencing my personality. Most importantly, I'm called to help others grow and that will not change. With my conditions and challenges, I will continue to preach to myself and help others grow just as God has instructed me to.

My journey is misunderstood because I smile and give the appearance that makes people feel that I know no pain.

Amid everything that I've been through, I would not change anything, and God knows that it has been rough. I see something in mine and I wonder, "What do you see in your misunderstood journey?"

DARREN PHELPS

CHAPTER SIX

LOOKING IN THE MIRROR

> *"If I didn't define myself for myself, I would be crunched into other people's fantasies for me and eaten alive."*
>
> *Audre Lorde*

Eventually, I arrived at that point in my life where I had to live for myself. Authenticity suddenly became a core value to me regardless of how many persons were on the line. With three children, the oldest 5 years old, there was more to live for in the world than I ever had.

Like most divorces, my divorce with Carol had a series of heated arguments. These debacles caused severe emotional bruises that drained me. We debated and fought about almost everything. Apparently, we had conflicting perspectives on most issues. One of the major arguments that we had was about our kids. While we agreed on the necessity for the children to have essential supplies to help them learn and grow faster, some other topics were hard nuts.

I would have sold my right foot to make sure my kids had everything they needed. They were my everything. My world revolved around my kids. I was doing everything I could to keep in contact with them, understand their challenges, and be there for them in ways that I was never given.

During our divorce hassles, my greatest fear was

losing the relationship I had with my kids. Dealing with the court battles, child support issues, and heated interactions made that time of my life almost unbearable. While we went through all that, my heart bled for my daughters. Children are the biggest victims or most damaged survivors of the events that occur when grown people can't seem to get their stuff together. I understood that Carol had a hard time giving up the kids, too. Perhaps, that was one thing we shared in common amid the rigors of court hearings. Those experiences were frustrating, embarrassing, and nerve-wracking.

My ministry was hit hard by the divorce as well. As soon as the news of my divorce went out, churches began to cancel my appointments. Presumably, they believed that a divorcee wasn't fit enough to teach the Gospel or pastor their congregation. The Progress-Index, the same Petersburg newspaper that featured preachers scheduled for sermons, started phoning and sending emails to inform me of canceled appointments.

The disappointment that came from the church's response to the marital challenge angered me. "Show me somewhere in the Bible that disqualifies me from being used by God because I'm a divorced man, a father, and minister," I said to church leaders in my local congregation. I never received an answer or response. Regardless of their inability to disqualify me from ministering, many people and churches still look down at me with a palpable level of disgust and disdain.

As the complicated process of my divorce with Carol went on, I couldn't get myself together. My fears magnified and my nerves tightened. With no harmful intent, I focused all those years on ministry and my children. I paid no attention to Carol's need for intimacy due to my obliviousness towards it. Looking back at the man in the mirror today, I see the things that I would have done differently. Learning how to be intimate and being teachable in areas outside your sphere of focus can be considered a vital quality to help marriages work.

For my ignorance, I owe plenty of apologies to Carol. Her attempts to bring us together was rewarded by my coldness. Our constant fights about the issue also revealed that we were not equipped to articulate, share, demand, or create the space in our lives for the other person. We had individual expectations that only showed up in counseling sessions but never materialized in the cause of the matrimony. Indeed, things are easier said than done when we rely on our might. Our miscommunicated expectations pushed us farther apart, faster than we would have ever imagined. With better, clearer communication, things would have been a lot better. Sadly, life happened.

Amid the fights, it was irking me to find out that we still disagreed on some things regarding our children. I believed that if there was anywhere we should share a common interest, it would be with the children. However, that wasn't the case. As we fought behind fallen curtains, we wore a brave look in public. It was difficult for anyone in church or within the neighborhood to predict accurately what was going on in our home. We showed up everywhere seemingly cheerful and attended events to honor our children wherever they were.

With all the frustration building up within, I spent time staring at the man in the mirror, realizing the slow changes from inside out. I found myself becoming attracted to other men. Before the divorce went through, however, I never got involved with one. I only admired and developed an interest in same-gender relationships long after Carol and I were separated. While married, I was living a full heterosexual life and honored my vows to Carol.

Regardless of the change in my sexual attraction, I'm not one of those 'DL preachers' because, at every point in time, I was certain and loyal to my sexual stand. I recognized gay people and also same-gender-loving people. I learned, from a very tender age, to respect people that were in different spectrums of gender expression and identity. Growing up in New York exposed me to various types of people and that was a benefit of once being a New Yorker.

As I discovered myself, I quietly began to love the person buried deep inside. Being gay was not something I ever asked God to take away. I kept it private because I knew there were many in my circle that would have made my life hell. Being a gay pastor was not going to fan well with many people in my life. Living my authentic self, meant destroying the images people had for and of me.

Although I had people around me that despised gays, I'm not in the best position to tell those stories. Carol always trusted me and had no reason to doubt my loyalty to her during our matrimony. As the kids grew up, she confirmed to them that our marriage was tough, and she did not receive the intimacy she often demanded. She and I discovered how ill equipped we were for marriage. I was unable to provide something to her that I needed for myself. Carol confirmed to my daughters our breakup was not the result of some scandal. She told them that we broke up for other reasons, mainly our miscommunicated expectations. Her truth was a wonderful gift.

After completing the divorce, I had the opportunity to explore my sexual identity while paying attention to what God was saying to me. It was a rough time in my life. I was unsure of myself and overall unsettled in many areas. At times, I thought I was attracted to women since it's the traditional thing to do. At other times, I was drawn to men. I tried dating other women which was great while we were friends. If they wanted more, I found myself in a panic and my insides would revolt. Even when I kissed other women, I never got that "spark". So, when I sensed they wanted more, I would just abruptly end it and flee.

Sadly, I used women so my ex-wife and church people would not label me as being "sick" or cast me to hell. To the strong, beautiful women I dated, I apologize. Had I been free, I would have never caused you pain.

As you read this book, I would assert that I had no history of being sexually abused in any way, by any gender. I understand that there are people that have suffered rape and they had to deal with it in some unpleasant way. I condemn such acts and empathize with the victims. However, that was not my story. My sexual identity wasn't defined by any form of unpleasant upbringing, experiences, or tragedies. It's just a part of my being and has come to be one that I accepted and embrace. I am created in the image of God!

Most times, as people question my "choice", they try to transpose the pains and guilt upon me. They ask to clarify whether I was abused or persuaded actively or passively as a child to have an interest in same-gender affairs. Inasmuch as I try to explain to them how it happened, I can't because I didn't choose it. It was simply an inevitable part of me. Who would consciously choose to be in a position where a lot of people question or hate you?

Embracing my personality and sexuality came with me declaring and expressing it clearly to the people around me. Carol didn't take it lightly. My daughters cried about it but eventually, we were cool and happy like the wonderful family that we've always been. Letting my mother know about my sexuality was yet another bridge to cross. She asked me directly and to my comfort, she reaffirmed her unwavering love and support. Once my fears of losing my children and mom were erased, I no longer feared what anyone else thought about who God made me! This was a pivotal moment in my journey.

The man in the mirror stared back at me after I had embraced myself. I saw the pains in his eyes dissipate and he hated himself less. His little smiles felt more genuine and he felt free. Even though I'd like to soar like the eagles in the sky, I remained private with everything that I'd discovered about myself, primarily because I loved my kids and I respected their lives and hoped that they would become adults to choose their lives and identities with little or no subtle influence from the things they witnessed during my journey. I love them and I always want(ed) them to be around comfortably. Today, I'm happy that they are all grown with families and have made their decisions respectively. Our bond is strong. I am blessed!

Looking in the mirror, I'm confident that I'm a decent father to my children and a strong faith leader. I stare at a man that has gone through life's struggles with great stories that will impact others in various spheres of life. Furthermore, regardless of the struggles and changes, I'm no less of a preacher, pastor, and lover of anyone else. God loves me and He had always confirmed that to me in more ways than one. And Apostle Paul reassures God's love for me and every one of us through his words: *"There is neither Greek nor Jew, neither slave nor free, nor is there male and female, for all are free in Christ Jesus."* (Eph. 3:28, NIV)

CHAPTER SEVEN

GIVING UP IS NOT AN OPTION

"The things that may have hurt you may have left scars, but they did not destroy you. You survived, and there is hope in that."

Bianca Sparacino

Of my more than 30 years of pastoral ministry. I've had experiences that have affected me, both positively and negatively.

Most of the experiences were meant to break me. I drew from the lessons and pain to help me stay strong. Through those lessons, I've correctly built my pastoral ministry. As much as we hunger to sort things out, things never get sorted out, at least not entirely. Life is a trial-and-error training ground. Do not let the errors stop you from trying because with each error, your next trial is a better attempt.

My theology was born out of pain. Indeed, God draws us out of a place of dejection to the peak, where nothing but his glory will be evident. From the scripture, the people mandated by God to achieve greatness were from the dumps with no chances of being at the peak.

While theologians that I've observed spur from healings, vision, clarity, and prosperity of their journeys, I was different in some ways that make me marvel at the wonders of God. Mine was born out of the ambiguity of my life from the beginning. In the grey areas of my life,

God still holds my hand, calls me His friend and son. He never left me the way I was. He helped me get through all the challenges that life threw at me and ensured that I remained faithful and on the right path.

Ministry comes with its highs and lows. However, in my case, there were more highs than lows. While the highs are thrilling to remember, I found the lows more impactful and educational. We learn from the down sides of our experiences and emphasize them to make sure we never make those wrong decisions again. Instead of feeding you on my highs, I'd rather share my lows, hoping they positively impact you.

My faith was tested, often. Being under attack from people I cared about was one of my low points. When people turn cold and do not reciprocate the energy you give to them, it can be demoralizing. Nevertheless, it is a part of life and we all must face it. I have been through it and God has kept me in His loving arms and has helped me recover from each crashing episode.

My commitment to a monogamous relationship with a guy turned out to produce one of the most demeaning results. We built together for several years, sharing everything with the utmost transparency. We lived together, bought a home, went through sickness, financial challenges, family drama, and pains of death, and still constantly hungered for intimacy.

We had years of what I believe was a solid

relationship. I truly loved him and was willing to do whatever it took to express that. However, A gap emerged between us as he grew quieter. He began making abrupt decisions without consulting me. His lack of attention towards our relationship was increasing and I wasn't feeling the energy. I was left wondering what could be wrong. Effective communication is imperative to building a solid relationship. He tried to assure me he was okay or that that he was onboard, but it all just seemed like empty words during this critical time in our relationship.

After many years of building a life together, things began to quickly go south. I became perplexed by his lack of balance between his friends and events and home. He and I spent hours discussing our future and where we saw God leading us. Each new path required a healthy risk and dedicated sacrifices, none of which I believe he was willing or capable of doing. While I give him credit for putting on a brave front, when it was time to walk into the newness, his lack of actions created challenges in our relationship.

During our final year together, I had to own a few harsh realities: there were many unresolved conflicts with his mother; he was selfish; we spoke about the "next" but never had true covenant; he was in covenant with his friends and events; and he was not emotionally available! Make no doubt about it, I loved him deeply! My love was not strong enough to weather such a significant change.

During my therapy sessions I realized I was guilty of connecting with similar people throughout my journey.

That spoke more about what I allowed or was attracted to then who was attracted to me. I kept counting on our love and commitment to override his fear of change and sacrifice. I was gravely mistaken. There were too many outside influences that blocked his ability to see beyond the cost of our next move. This is not about competition with friends; it's about making time for things that are important and give you pleasure.

There were times when our anger caused us to have very painful verbal exchanges. That final year was unlike all the years we shared. Yet, it was a critical time for me to rediscover deeper unhealed places. I rediscovered that I often connected with people that had tempers and outbursts. Remember my childhood? The times of violence and how I coped were still playing out in my adult relationships. My unhealthy practice of keeping silent or waiting until I had enough... had grown unbearable.

I moved on to the next phase of my life alone with all the bruises from our relationship showing on the surface and defining me in the face of life. He didn't show up when I was installed into my new position in ministry, even after I extended the invitation. It was glaring and his message was clear that I was no longer needed. I felt used and abused. His actions revealed his true character, which I thought I had known. It became clear that he didn't want us to build a life together. If I had done something wrong, he never gave me a chance to make it right.

Ironically, the things I asked of him were the same

things Carol asked of me. Inasmuch as I wasn't capable of giving her what she needed at the time, I certainly wasn't abusive to her. My fights with Carol were a lot more mature. Our transparency and loyalty to each other were admirable.

With him, I never gave up on what God had said to me and was still saying to me. I had to continue moving in line with God's instruction. Needless to say, I wished I had enough time to unpack the experiences. I've moved on in my healing process, I forgave him (mostly), and God has been unconditionally faithful.

Giving up is not an option for me and shouldn't be for anyone. While I went through various challenges in my personal life, the ministry had its roadblocks, as well. Church leaders organized against me. They issued false claims and lied against me to detract me from ministry, which caused a whirlwind in my life because I followed God's instructions and embraced my identity. I faced these challenges in good faith and believed that they are launchpads into greater places that God has prepared for me.

At every moment in our lives, we are required to make sacrifices before we can advance to the next level of our career and life. In ministry, God requires the same from me and every other minister of the Word. I do not know what sacrifices are required of me but with each encounter I face, I stay focused on God, trading off whatever I had to remain on the path that He has assigned me to follow.

Along the line, I've been mocked, rejected, lied on, misused, and most of all misunderstood. I may understand why those ministers and other church leaders revolted against me and conspired to push me off my pastoral career. However, I do not understand the rationale behind their beliefs that I'm not qualified to follow God. Regardless, it makes more sense to me that they took those actions and made the decisions because they didn't care about me or humanity. They were more concerned about their income. Getting rid of me was the best way to make that happen. Church and politics have always been intertwined from the inception. Nevertheless, a large portion of pastors and ministers shun the malpractice.

Silence, most times, is a virtue. In silence, your oppressors may assume you're near a breaking point. Although this may be the case for most persons who are fickle in the face of chaos, my silence is often misunderstood. It's in my silence I hear God's voice clearer, where I find a new resolve to press forward even at my weakest moments! I seek the face of God in everything that I do. I commit my challenges to His hands and bring my worries to His throne of grace. In silence, I stay closer to God and build my intimacy with Him. My faith has made me stronger and firmer at every point and helped me overcome the trials and tribulations that have come my way.

At the time, I didn't know what God had in store for

me. I didn't know where he was leading me. My ministry was quaking, relationship over and I trusted that from the chaos would come the liberation and my onset to greater heights.

It's sad to see people give up. Some give up because people reject them, cheat on them, betray them, or lie to them. There are several reasons why people give up. Even though these experiences seem like good reasons to quit, please don't. I've had all these things and more happen in my life and I strongly believe that God has footprints on my path and I'm following His lead.

By giving up, you miss all the possibilities the future has in store for you. You also settle for what you already know how it feels. Don't you want to explore your limitlessness? Are you willing to forfeit the glories of pursuing what your heart believes and what God has prepared for you because some people in your life don't see things the way you do? Please, give it another thought! Trust the process of living in your truth and purpose. It will guide you further.

One practice that really helped me navigate those difficult times were the notes that I wrote to myself. Because I'd adopted the practice of preaching to myself as those ministers at the Cathedral advised me, I make constant notes to myself. Consider writing notes to your future self. Regardless of your inclinations, studies have proven that writing notes and keeping letters to yourself have a huge impact on your mental wellbeing and resilience.

My commitment, uncompromised standards, unwillingness to abandon the journey through ministry, life, love and friendship have been helpful. The process has given me a stubbornness that the scriptures support. *"Therefore, my dear brothers and sisters, stand firm. Let nothing move you. Always give yourselves fully to the work of the Lord, because you know that your labor in the Lord is not in vain."* 1 Corinthians 15:58

Listen, I have had several death threats. I have had moments where people came into the church and dropped off letters saying that I am sending people to hell. I have had people who came back to me and blamed me for their failures and their struggles. I have also seen people come into my home and try to disrupt it. There is so much more I could share, but still, giving up was not an option. My goal remains to try to live my life to honor God.

My journey through life is indeed misunderstood. Dealing with fellow church members who created drama or coming home and your spouse has his bags packed and going out of town with a "friend", made me re-examine the foundation of my beliefs. I believe it has love at its core. However, the behaviors that I observed from people over time makes me assume that the definition of love is relative. And of course, it isn't. Love is pure and can't be assumed to mean otherwise.

You must not care what life throws on you. You must

not care how others believe God works because He works in unique ways. Worry less about how God will use the people around you to take you to new heights. Once you get the truth about who you are and where God is leading you, stand firm, and embrace your journey. Hold your head up and believe that God has you in His heart. It doesn't matter how people see you from the outside because we are all in the middle of our own MISUNDERSTOOD JOURNEY. Keep going as God leads, and always remember that GIVING UP IS NOT AN OPTION!

ABOUT THE AUTHOR

Rev. Dr. Darren W. Phelps grew up in Queens, NY. He is well known as a community activist, educator, and a nonprofit senior executive. Darren is a much sought-after conference speaker, lecturer, and preacher. His career spans 30 years. He is ordained clergy in the Christian Church (Disciples of Christ) denomination. Darren, a graduate of Virginia State University and United Theological Seminary, Certificate Black Theology Princeton Theological Seminary, has served churches in Virginia, Florida, and Washington, D.C. He has two daughters and five grandchildren. Darren spends his free time traveling, watching cartoons, and exploring new foods and customs. For more information, visit www.drdarrenphelps.com.

DARREN PHELPS

www.ingramcontent.com/pod-product-compliance
Lightning Source LLC
Chambersburg PA
CBHW071152090426
42736CB00012B/2303